Poetry from another *world*

Neya B

بسم الله

From me
to
you.

<u>Author's note</u>

I have a little message for you, my loves. First, I wanted to thank you. Thank you for making this dream real and pushing me forward.

Then, I published this book only for pleasure. I don't want to have any questions about my health or else. If my words can help some, and some others, to express their thoughts, it is enough for me.

Yes, this collection is heavy because it contains years of thought, emotion, and reflection that I have had. This collection is not here to worry you.

This book allows me to give you a part of me that remained locked up and with whom I made peace a long time ago.

If you are ready to read this kind of topic, go ahead. Otherwise, please read the list below to give you an idea.

<u>Trigger warnings</u>

- Suicide
- ED (eating disorder)
- SA (sexual assault)
- Grooming (psychological manipulation of a child to sexually abuse them)

- Non-consent
- Dissociation
- Mutilation
- Body dysmorphia

For broken souls

like me

These thoughts absorb me.
Lifeless like an orb.
Fed by the past.
My dreams were a blast.

Will they erase this monochrome world?
The one you painted me with
every atom.

Enchanted or unhappy world.
Exposing our fragile bodies.
Making us fearful.

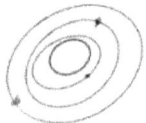

I would like to be near you.

Facilitating my transition to the other side.

أفكار مدمرة...

Love.
Love.
Love.

What is love ?

Is it that fiery feeling?
Internally liquefying us.
Making our bodies extremely heavy.

So is this love?

Or does it make us stronger?
Blinding us to death.
Turning our bodies to dust.
Should we be proud of it?

ما هو الحب ؟
إنه شعور يعمينا.

There is no order in my words.
Thoughts, heavy thoughts.
That's all I'm made of.

How to make sense of them?
If when you see me
I am drowning.

I built these walls.

That you try to break.

Wanting so much to reveal,
This well-hidden side of me.

This alexandrine doesn't make you keen.
But in a few lines, your soul comes to life,
Leaving your heart full in a restrained world.

The melody that unites you.
Binding your souls with one voice.
You who are gathered here.
Leaving me alone all at once.

I would like to share this melody.
No longer be a spectator of this life.
To be part of this disunited world.

Yet here I am alone, face down.
Praying at night when my heart is blank.

نجد دائمًا طريقة لإضافة بعض الألوان إلى
قلوبنا الفارغة.

On our way to Allah,
You used to squeeze my hand tightly.
But now you're gone.
I see no tomorrow anymore.

I tried to imagine my heart full.
Yet, it doesn't change anything.

Without you, I can no longer live.

So, on this carpet, I surrender.

Letting my tears fall until I choke.

Will HE be able to make me forget?
Change this far too great pain.
Will HE be able to help me move forward?
Making my body move by HIS commands.

This weak body is hanging by a thread.
But I only have this sentence in mind:

ٱلْحَمْدُ لِلَّهِ

The return of this unusual feeling.
Isn't it strange?
It's just turmoil.
When does that change?

Your soul that was once bound to mine.

Here I am, no longer yours.

أفتقدك .

Live, live, live…

When did this change to "survive"?

I thought I could escape it.
But now I find myself stuck.
All these horrible ordeals,
Make me believe in possible outcomes.

I wouldn't want to think about it…
That open window.
I've been staring at it for years.
An emotion discovered.

Sometimes I imagine the wind blowing the
curtains,

After my body has gone through it.

"Hope dies last."

I kept repeating this sentence,
Thinking it would just be a phase.
HE who gave back my soul every morning,
Couldn't HE see my great sorrow?

These thoughts made me fragile like a vase.
Without even tasting this ecstatic life,
I thought of the pleasures of this testing
world.
This ephemeral joy that we all find.

This دُنْيا doesn't bring out the best in me.
I dream of getting away from it to be with YOU.

هذه الدنيا امتحان وإغراء.

Why leave when you can stay?
Am I not good enough to attract you?
This greedy world makes me unhappy.
Without you by my side, I'm very fearful.
I was always told not to rely on anyone,
But how to tell them that you were *that* soul?
This soul that I selected.
Whereas I am just a simple woman.

A woman you left for dead.
And now that I'm strong enough,
You dare show me your face?
Time hasn't made you wise.

With a sly smile.

I'll send you back to where you came from.

Goodbye, sadness.

I'm much better off without you.

Be satisfied,
That's what I want.
Without being perfect.
Or making you happy.

I want to focus on myself.
To stop thinking about you.

This simple idea.

Seems to be the most complicated of all.

Being alone at home.
Or surrounded by my friends.
I have the same feeling.
Solitude is my company.

This empty heart that I hold out to you
Gives my soul this absence.
How to come back to this moment?
This time when it beat without latency.

"You learned to say no?"
So, don't you accept my refusal?
Is it always the same song?
Your orders must *be* without any denial?

However, I am human like you.

Why would you have the right to?

But I'm refused my right.

ظلم.

This howl of pain that no one hears.
It just echoes on these white walls
That I color with my voice.
Yet, no one notices.

What should I do to be remarked?

This thought comes from this forgotten child.

يبدو أن عواء الألم هذا أبكم.

Your laughter, I remember them.
Thinking it was support.
Even if they are in the past,
Nothing can erase them.

Sometimes I still dream about it.

Those smiles pursue me to death.

Even in my nightmares, I feel their presence.

You who thought it was trivial.
Here I am followed by these petty laughs.

This restraint I had with YOU
Made me sad every time.
I wanted to move forward to find YOU.
But now I'm stuck.

Lost between these two sides,
I no longer know where to set foot.

So, in this confusion,
I return to my lessons.

NEYA B

These poems are in a way intended to you.
Blacks on paper, giving you a part of me.
I write them sometimes to heal myself.
But, I now understand that I needed YOU.

You who read these few words,
I hope to help your soul.
Soothing, your pain too
Without anyone blaming you.

In this suffocating world.

I am often denied access to YOUR house.
I find that completely immoral.
But for some, all of this is normal.

How can I evolve,
If I am prevented from moving forward?

المساجد مفتوحة للجميع.

Together for better and for worse.

However, the worst only comes from you.

Why do I always end up binging?
I eat, but it doesn't seem like enough.
I cut everything to come back to zero.

But I'm the first one at the table to finish.

You shower me with gifts.
Thinking you could keep me.

But nothing seems to work.

هداياك لن تغير أي شيء.

Why is it easier to forgive him?

When he didn't ask.
But you who look so much like me

I can't forget those moments.

So be patient.

Maybe one day, I'll get there.

The abyss reaches out to me.
I still find myself at the bottom.
They make me believe that I can go up.
Still, I'm only digging.

In this tomb, I see my reflection.
It makes me shiver with regret.

How can I save myself?

"قَالَ لَا تَخَافَآ إِنَّنِى مَعَكُمَآ أَسْمَعُ وَأَرَىٰ"

S20; V46

Thanks to YOU, I'm no longer afraid.

These oppositions were supposed to stop you.
So why did you keep going?

— *From this broken child.*

Buying my silence is vain,

Because HE hears and sees everything.

These scars keep burning me
When I see them in the mirror.
I would like to erase them.
Yet I always hide them in my drawer.

They who made ink flow.

This red ink stained my clothes.

That absent smile that you love so much

Ended up disappearing.

Because I can't pretend anymore.

NEYA B

I like to play, I love to play.

By your side, I only lose.

This incompatibility broke us.

All those hot tears you caused.
And, I'm still ready to forgive you.

Your impatience has destroyed me.
I wasn't completely ready.

Didn't you see it?

You, who forced me to take the first step.

"*Do it for me.*"
"*If you love me, do it.*"
"*I no longer matter to you?*"

"*I'm not asking you for too much.*"

Your sentences are on repeat in my head.

And even if I politely refuse,
Your words will make me look bad.
So, I finally accept your requests.

ألمتني ...

Constant lag with reality.

How can I find YOU?

Time passes so fast.
I lost myself.
Your book invites me.
I return your right.

I don't need all these questions.

I'm learning to live with it.
To pay no more attention.

NEYA B

This macabre world

Doesn't make me want to stay.
With my eyes, I saw you coming.

Since that day, I've been untouched.

I would like to detach myself from this image,
But I only see her, it's a shame.

Thinking myself was away from this filth,
I'm getting closer to this mischief.

Marked my body forever.

Or face this imperfect reflection.
Unfortunately, the choice is quickly made.

My gaze rests on this mirror.

Reality distorter.

Announcer of many truths.

Abandon is a part of me.
This promise to stay every time,
I don't believe it anymore.
But I'm still begging you to stay.

My burnt knees can attest.

My oppositions did not make you back down,

You who thought you were entitled to everything.
Here I am devastated.

Evidences were right under your nose,
But none of this seems to prove it.
What should I do to be believed?
Are these red marks not enough for you?

I'm now distraught,
Me, who thought I had you as allies.

Why, why, why?
That's what I ask myself every time.
Unfortunately, I was chosen
To be this bruised soul.

I'm a tested soul.

Only YOU can help me.

ا يُكَلِّفُ ٱللَّهُ نَفْسًا إِلَّا وُسْعَهَا.

S2; V286

Writing is medicine for me.

You, did you find it?
Are you still looking for it?
How much time did you spend?

Why stay in this comfort?

Don't you want to be cured?

This music that I constantly heard,

Replaced YOU for a time.

I'm sorry.

توبوا إلى الله.

I'm the scapegoat for your anger.
As soon as there is a defect, I am the overhang.
Each time, you tell me it's the last.
But yet, I still cure each of your regrets.

I say it's not me
But no one believes me.

Even though that child is now gone.

Why didn't anyone believe me?

Question from a child.

My soul returns every morning
To face this teasing world.
I pray to pass this test,
Just to prove myself.

"*You do this for attention.*"

Excuse me for hurting myself.

— *From this little girl who had to learn to take care of herself.*

NEYA B

This long alexandrine will never have

Pieces of the past,
Comes back to haunt me.

I thought I had turned the page,
But I find myself in this cage.
Even after all these years,
I'm still trying to figure out how to move forward.

تقدم دون التراجع.

Allah gave me back my taste for life.
HIM who found my dried-up soul.

Otherwise, I wouldn't be here.
Yet HE was only a step away.

لا تفقد الامل ابدا.

My heart vibrates at your side,
This simple feeling warms me.
I wouldn't want to forget it,
Without overdosing on it.

You will forever be my other half.

NEYA B

Just for fun.

NEYA B

Saving you would have been easy.
But how to go back to the past?
Protect you from those hands that changed you?
In an instant, you became fragile…

Re-appropriating it has left its mark.
Since then, you no longer feel in your place.

Excuse me for letting you down.

If I had resisted, would you be able to breathe?

I'm sorry.

Now you are twenty years old, and HE has
appeased you.

أسامحني.

Pride is just a state.
Forgiveness is just an action.
"Sorry" is just a word.

So why don't you use it?

إنه بسيط مع ذلك.

I go forward with the feeling of going backwards.
The further I go, the further I return on my steps.

Am I really making progress?
To forget you?
To erase you?

You, the pain that makes me wobble.

I perceive, yet I feel nothing.

How did I manage to dissociate my heart from reality?
Am I trapped by this dimension?
Sometimes I wish I could find that connection again.
Her who could make me shiver just by a look.

Now I'm just disconnected.
No longer able to separate my feelings from this constant black fog.

I love you from as far back as I can remember.
I will love you until my soul rises to heaven.

Love is a disease that weakens our hearts.
We don't decide who we fall in love with, but we
can decide to take the leap.

Live
and
Die

Sadly, these words don't rhyme,
Because, inside, they do.

If to live means suffering, then I prefer dying.

You see, deep down, they end up rhyming.

العيش أثناء المعاناة يشبه التنفس كما لو كنت
ميتًا بالفعل.

This world is all about harmony and balance.
You only need a few words to find your meaning.

This is a blank page.
Empty of ink, but filled with thoughts.
Is it really a blank page if I keep talking?

When will it be full enough to be considered a
page?

I don't know.
    I don't know.
        I don't know.
            I don't know.
            I don't know.
                I don't know.

I write, but I still have space, yet if we look down
again, this is still a blank page. But, once the
eyes are skyward, it is filled with words that
seem to make sense.
It's up to you how you see it.

"*I am proud of you!*"

Words that I would have liked to hear from you.

Were they too heavy to say?
Or... am I just not worth it?

Disappointment is all I see.
I've changed, but no one notices.
You still judge me by my past mistakes.
Can't you see that this monster is erased?

Why constantly reminding me of the missing
person that I was?
Aren't you proud of the woman in front of you?

Am I still that monster you hate?

Am I really *me*?

I watch my memories like a new TV show.
No emotion comes from me, I am totally
disconnected from it.
To see this child who is being described to me.
But is she really who I am?

I don't know.

Would you like me to be her?
Prude, amiable, obedient and frail?

I'm not that child you idealize.

I am me.
Broken, damaged, destroyed.
I am me.
The one I rebuilt.
Me.

At least…
I believe.

أوهام أو ذكريات ، لم أعد أعلم.

Your words hurt me.
How to make you notice it?
Because when you see me, I am only joy.

Comments, comments, and always comments.

I no longer want to feel this red ink that you pour on my skin in order to rectify ~~your~~ my mistakes.

You make me feel hate, but how do I spit it out on someone who's supposed to protect me?

You are the one who must make me better, but how to discern good behavior from bad, when you yourself are not well?

I'm not...
I must not...
I would not be...
And I should never,

(Be) An extension of you.

I draw closer to HIM.
HIM who guided and soothed me.
Without HIS words, I wouldn't be.
So what more can we say than:

اَللّٰهُ أَكْبَر

When I was younger, I thought I was alone in
this world.
I thought HE hated me, seeing my life crumble
before my eyes.

I was told: "*If you are punished, it is because
you have done wrong.*"

When I had done nothing.

How to love YOU, if I am made to believe in this
injustice?
But one simple sentence changed everything.

"Your Lord has neither abandoned you nor hated
you." [S93; V3]

"*Love has no age.*"

You who saw a woman.
Yet, I was only a child.

By reading the Quran, I learned to love YOU.
By understanding it, I have learned to do what
YOU love.

But when I do wrong, I have this doubt that grips
me, repeating to myself:

"*O Allah, will YOU still love me if I sin?*"

So I open this book that I hold so dear, and I
read.
I read until I see these words that answer my
questions.

حبي لك لا ينكسر.

"You eat too much."
I'm listening to you.
"You're not eating enough."
I'm lost.
Is it too much or not enough?

However, the only feedback I heard was made up of the words "fat", "fatty", "obese", "problems"...

But now that you see my past self, I wasn't?

Have you forgotten?
Not my case.

I remember your words, your remarks, your suggestions, everything.
Absolutely everything.

Couldn't you just help me?
Or...
Were you also lost between too much and not enough?

I wish I had a good relationship with you.
You are destroying me, but I am patient.
I only have a while before I can love you.

I was made to hate you.
I'm sorry.

Patience.
I will come to love you.

For me, in a few years.

"Love yourself" & *"Speak yourself"*

Words that I give to you, and that were given to me by people I love from the bottom of my heart.

I purple you.

Whore.

That's what you called me.
Only once, though…

It was only enough that one time to mark me
forever.

One insult, two insults, three insults.
At the end of the umpteenth, I decided not to
count anymore.

By creating this barrier, I was able to protect
myself.

.

Narcissus died due to his love for himself.
Do I have to love you to death to prove my love?

Or do I let you go and never see you come
back?

Is this also proof that love is deadly?
Whether for a person or for ourselves?

العشق.

Am I really impure with this blood flowing?
Or am I just a human like you?

All these contradictions have lost this child of
yesteryear.

She was hiding to remove her impurities.
We were not taught to love, but to fear being
judged.

All it takes is a simple encounter to change everything.

This angel fallen from heaven soothes my soul, soothes my overwhelming thoughts without even knowing it.

I am tired.

It's a phrase I repeated to myself for a long time.
Mechanically, it turned into:

You will make it.

I am often compared to the sun, making my
loved ones laugh.
Bringing them that missing light.
But, what about me?

In fact, I understand.

This is a fiery star, warming souls and hearts.
The planets revolve around it, needing it.

In the end, it always finds itself alone,
surrounded by these beautiful worlds.

تحترق الشمس وحدها في هذا الكون الشاسع.

NEYA B

ABCDEFGHIJKLMNOPQRSTUVWXYZ

26 letters.

However, this is never enough.

ا ب ت ث ج ح خ د ذ ر ز س ش ص ض ط
ظ ع غ ف ق ك ل م ن ه و ي

حروف ٢٨

ومع ذلك، هذا لا يكفي أبدا

Love is beautiful.
A unique, mysterious feeling for me.

We can handle most of our emotions, yet love
remains uncontrollable.

This wild feeling makes you vibrate, but,
personally, it scares me...
Because I fear failure.

Your colors are so transparent.
Flowing through your pores, letting me see your
emotions without even questioning you.
You are easy to understand and analyze.

However, I still can't talk to you.

"*No.*"

That's enough.
I don't need to add any explanation.
No reasons.
Nor emotion.

"*No*" is an answer.

ץ

Smoking kills, they say.

So why didn't they keep their promise?

Happiness is fleeting.
But next to YOU, it seems eternal to me.

That smile that makes you so happy fades in difficult times.
I can't hold this mask together anymore, so I pull away as it evaporates in my hands under those endless tears.

أحيانًا تكون الدموع أعلى من صوت الكلمات.

Sexualization does a lot of damage, but when
are we going to realize it?

Patience.
You can do it.

*— For this child that I would have liked
to save*

The scars fade over time.
Yet, I can never really forget.

Our souls are compatible.
Everything led us to be together.
Nevertheless, our actions that have bruised
them, prevent us from being reunited.

This feeling weakens me.
As soon as he appears, I lose control.
These endless tremors remind me of how
introverted I am.

I speak, yet no one understands me.
Should I use another language?

Suis-je comprise ?

هل أنا مفهوم؟

이해할 수 있습니까?

Still not?
I'm quite annoyed...

Should I be mute forever?
Perhaps silence will have a better effect.

My social battery is depleted.
I don't know how to tell you that.
So, I'm standing there waiting.

These cuts on my body make me stagger, but
what a pleasure they make me feel when
finished.

Traveling makes me dream.

Living in a world different from yours when it is only a few kilometers from yours, it's incredible, isn't it?

What is this body that I see in my mirror?
Is it really mine?
Why can't I accept it?

I would love to draw it my way, but year after
year it still hasn't changed.

I'm tired of worrying about it.

This XXXL sweater will be able to hide the
damage, then.

This cage made of glass, I would like to break it
just to join you on the other side.

We, who were one, are now divided.

This pride blocks your words.
Wouldn't you like to give it up to make us
progress?

After so many years, I finally admit defeat.
Leaving you while I keep on going.

الكبرياء مرض قاتل.

"*I love you.*"

I would like to mean it.
Feel it.
Yet, I can't do so until I'm able to think it for
myself.

Am I really selfish if I put myself first?
If I put my needs before yours?
Am I a monster if I no longer want to share your sorrows?

No.

So why do you make me feel like one?

Poetry from another world

Acknowledgments

Thank you to my family and loved ones for the support shown. Many of these pages had been locked away in my iPhone notes for years now. I finally had the courage to take the plunge by taking inspiration from a friend to put them together and do something with them. At first, I doubted publishing it, but seeing that these words could help some people to move forward in their journey (spiritual or personal) just by finding themselves in one of my texts, made me rethink this idea.

Then there it is.

Thank you for the support you show me when you see me starting a project. I'm incredibly lucky to have you. Thank you so much. There is a tiny possibility that this little book will end up in your hands before my next projects, just to make you wait a little longer behind your screens/books. I look forward to seeing your feedback on my texts, as well as your opinions. This poetry collection was quickly finished because a good part was already written.

One day there may be enough for a second part…

الله أعلم

I love you, be strong.
And a good cry always feels good.

Now it's up to you to turn the page.

www.ingramcontent.com/pod-product-compliance
Lightning Source LLC
Chambersburg PA
CBHW051633120626
46551CB00014B/2059